Soaring Higher

Michael Bobb

Soaring Higher

With photographs

by

the author

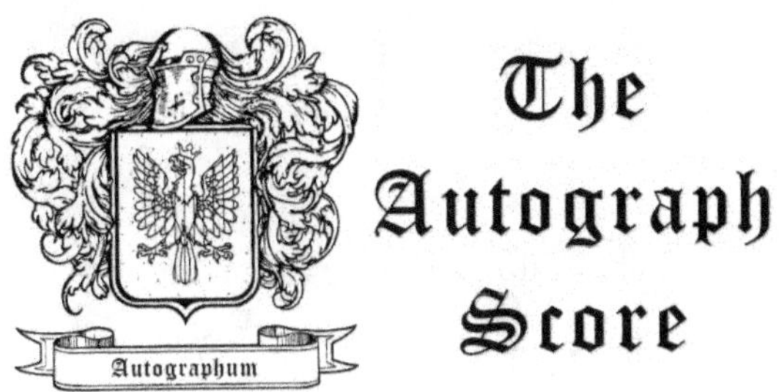

First published in 2023
by The Autograph Score
www.theautographscore.co.uk

1

Paperback
ISBN 978-1-7392947-0-0

E-book
ISBN 978-1-7392947-1-7

The Autograph Score, London
theautographscore@outlook.com

"Words are potent.
Why keep good ones to yourself. . .?"

TABLE OF CONTENTS

LIST OF PLATES

INTRODUCTION

- 13 -

Splish, splash, splosh!   This book is the result of what happens when my right hemisphere throws ink about! Poetry is, I consider, an artistic pursuit; an activity that uses one's unique thought processes to select specific words which express and articulate in a particular way that is distinct from other genres of literature. The whole process of writing poetry cannot necessarily be explained. On some occasions I have a title, sometimes not. Sometimes I have a clear idea what I am going to write, sometimes the idea is less than clear. Sometimes I research, sometimes it is not necessary. In quite a large majority of cases I simply aim my pen at the page, and a poem appears! For a more detailed explanation I suggest consulting a friendly neuroscientist!

Art and creativity is an essential part of my life. You could say it is my personal definer in many respects – including visual art. Some years after reading an area of visual media at Sussex University, I discovered the world of computerised image manipulation – this lead to many enjoyable hours playing with image-editing software. My output includes: enhancing photographs, graphic designs and creating abstract images. For this book, I have decided to include a selection of black and white photographs.

In this tapestry of poems there is a thread that occasionally becomes visible: music. Examples of where music lives and breathes are found in the rhyming poems, i.e. similar phonic sounds, as well as poems where a musical lexicon has been simply weaved into the literature. This idea has also been taken to a lateral level, marrying specially selected music with performances of the poems. You can now find the happy couple living in a land that never ends...

"If you were inside a Tardis, what would you do?

Open the door and go out.

Let's open the door. . ."

Soaring, Soaring Higher And Higher

Soaring, soaring higher and higher
From here I can see for mile upon mile
Far over the seas to the horizon
Come with me and stay a while

As we ride the ascending thermals
Or take advantage of the wind
All it takes is just a moment
As we leave our cares behind

No one will notice as we take our flight
Soon we will be far, far away
Where the Earth has stopped spinning
And there is always the light of day

Just close your eyes and you will know
The gentle call from inside your heart
Everyone around us won't see a thing
And this will be our journey's start

Deeper and deeper, only joy exists
This vision can see the end of infinity
Onward and upward the innermost calls
Can you see us, can you see?

Wave upon wave the thermals come
Its warmth takes us further on
Effortlessly we keep on rising
Like hot air in the summer's sun

Things past, present and future are one
A singularity where all tenses merge
The sight we have has no boundaries
Our perspectives do not converge

A fresh wind is approaching
Our countenance grows at the sight
There are others too in her midst
Oh what pleasure, what delight

The encounter is exhilarating
This feeling will never, ever, cease
Everything physical falls away
How great this sweet release

...All we feel is light
...All we hear is light
...All we taste is light
...All we see is light

The light is all around us
The light pervades us
The light emits from us
There is nothing but light

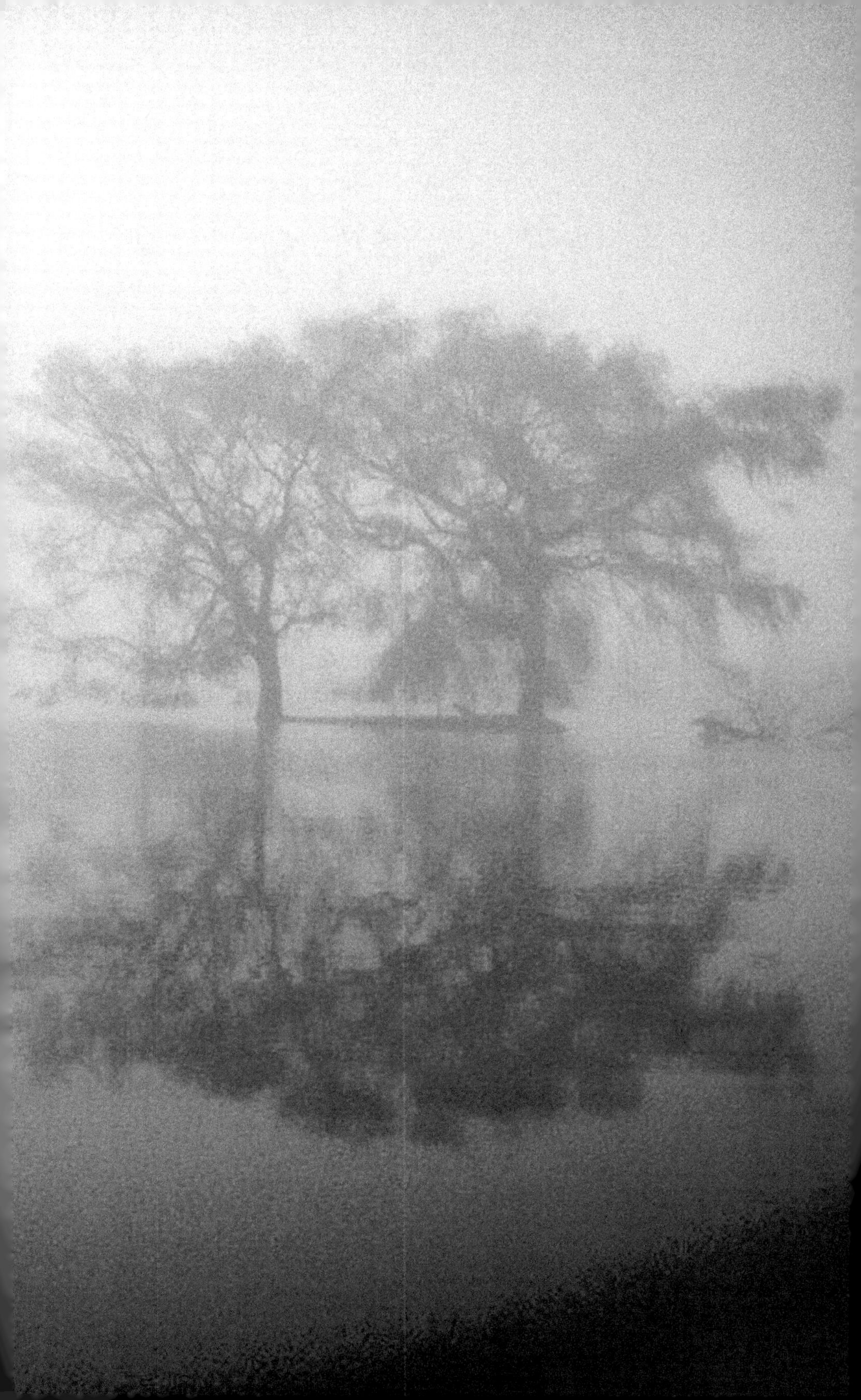

The Sky, The Sky

The sky, the sky in all its many shades of blue
Spectacled scientists tell us it has to be this hue
Much praise, I think, to them is certainly due

This first poem is dedicated to someone called Huw
A special, dear and loyal friend who has a pet ewe
And I reckon he could be the next Doctor Who

When I am out and about sometimes I stand, as you do
Or indoors and pass by a window and look through
I look at the sky, so infinite... so harmonious... so true...

I have experienced the sky, and to use words would be words too
few
The first and second heavens disappeared as I flew
And I discovered a place I know but never knew

In this trilogy one more poem follows part two
Then these three will bid you, "farewell, goodbye, adieu"
Leaving you to look at the sky and enjoy the view

GOD CREATES

God creates
Heaven, sky
Beasts below
Feathered fly

God exhales
Into man
Adam, Eve
Eden's jam

Christ descends
Perfect life
Jesus dies
Xtra strife

Jesus lives
Hades coughs
Christ ascends
Far above

Riding clouds
Christ returns
People see
People learn

Souls saved
Death dies
New Earth
New sky

Baroque jewels
Gold, jasper
Clear crystal
Life, water

Fruitful tree
People come
Lasting light
Divine home

Jesus weds
Betrothed Church
Spirit calls
Angels search

Omni God
Thrice Una
Alpha and
Omega

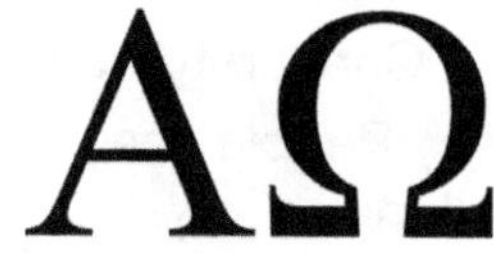

What Is There In All Creation...?

What is there in all creation that can compare to the sky?
She, at times, can be quite calm as well as electrifying
Also, sometimes, conveys sadness and happiness — quite
confusing
This is because she is pure and 3 times very high

She has an air of nobility and quality of the highest order
Affluence, excellence and distinction – affirmative, certainly
Royalty quickly comes to mind – yes, aristocracy
If one were to choose a gemstone, it would be blue sapphire

The sky has other qualities too, such as eternity
She is all optimistic and invisibly strong
The distance from here to her is never long
She is faithfully associated with Christianity

If you have confidence and a little concentration
If you aim for the sky or go beyond your limit
If you rest assured that the everlasting God is in it
Then contemplating her will satisfy the imagination

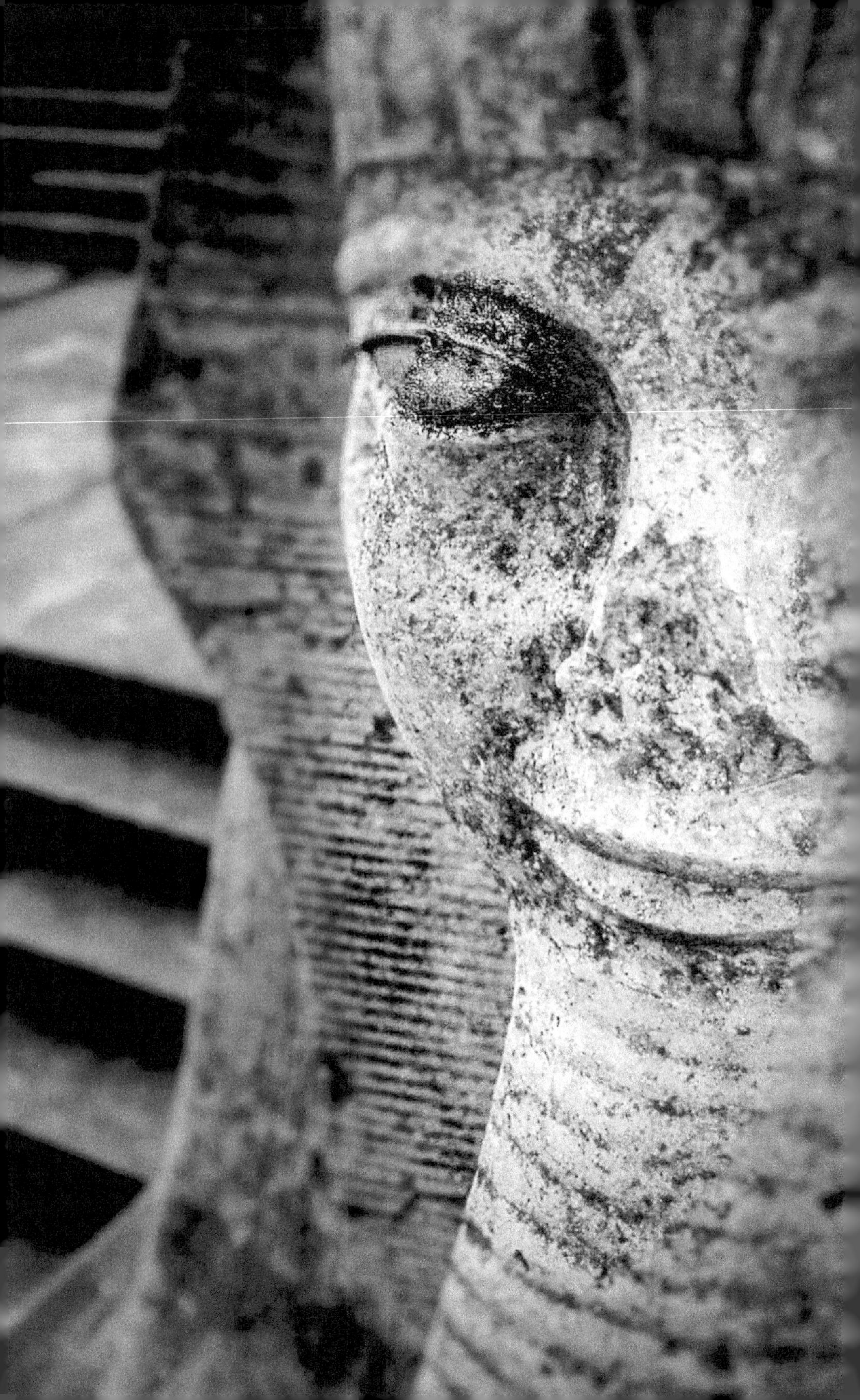

I Have A Nikon Camera

I have a Nikon camera
That captures photons new
The light sensitive sensor
Is sharp, accurate and true

The many megapixels
Facilitates detailed photography
Allowing tight cropping of images
Just check your computer's memory

My finely tuned Nikon
Is like my artistic eye
It works out visual compositions
Like the square root of pi

It records the physical world
In the flash of a second
Nothing can escape its gaze
All situations it can comprehend

It always preserves privacy
Is honourable through and through
Always upholds dignity
And may even flatter you

It can make you see the world
Like no one has ever before
Its perspectives are quite different
Always true, always pure

Squeeze the shutter release
And time will be frozen
Never ageing, never fading
Just fresh and ever golden

My Nikon is full of suggestions
Telling me how it should go
Not like this or like that
But: you know, you know, you know

My Nikon catches the occasion
And atmospheres that are visceral
Whether the emotions are high or low
Its lens is always visible

It can make you laugh and smile
Have you rolling in comic agony
Make you giggle until tickled pink
Much, much more than the comic Dandy

My Nikon has other feelings too
Like when your heart strings are plucked
And you're overtaken with emotion
Drawing tears from your eye duct

Sometimes it uses colour
As vibrant as a prism's hues
Sometimes they are muted, though
Akin to richer and sophisticated truths

Sometimes it uses black and white
To tell a documentary story
Or to claim a fine art status
In the nation's pre-eminent gallery

...And when my Nikon is resting
My computer's flame is lit
Bouncing pixels from program to program
With the imagination the only limit

Pennsylvania

(The Keystone State)

In 2017 I was sojourning in Ambleside. The American style B & B was named Compston House. I happened to be in the Pennsylvanian Suite which was well facilitated and included sufficient reading material — including information about Pennsylvania. From these facts and figures I extracted the following rhyming verse.

With a population @ 12,000,000
And total area over 46k square miles
Pennsylvania is really quite large
With many couples walking down the aisles

Its chief industries are all interesting
Biotechnology and advanced manufacturing
Agribusiness and travel and tourism
Healthcare and printing and publishing

Corn is one of Pennsylvania's chief crops
As well as hay and mushrooms as it goes
What has to be more important than these
Are winter wheat, apples and potatoes

A state motto is always a good thing to have
Stirring courage and feelings of togetherness
You may have one, or know one, or able to quote one
Pennsylvania's is: "Virtue, Liberty and Independence"

Pennsylvania's state flower is the Mountain Laurel
Research their medicinal information
And its state bird is the Ruffed Grouse
Also known as the Prairie Chicken

There are famous Pennsylvanians, too
Including Perry Como and Grace Kelly
Benjamin Franklin and Jimmy Stewart
And Andy Wharhol and Grace Kelly

Wrynose Pass

I'm on my way back to my lodgings
Not long, I hope, 'till I'm safely back
I set the SatNav and follow its commands
It's getting darker and will soon be pitch black

Directions take me along an unexpected route
There are no streetlights as I travel
And low clouds hide stars and moon
No cats eyes either, just miles of gravel

The SatNav tells me the way to go
You can trust its internal compass
They map out the quickest route
Then I hear it say, "Continue 9 miles on Wrynose Pass"

"Oh no!" I anxiously think to myself
"Wasn't there an accident not far from here
Traffic was redirected for quite a few miles
Oh dear… oh dear… oh dear...!"

Wrynose Pass is famously challenging
It is not a cruise down Oxford Street
It takes precision, technique and nerves of steel
To navigate this part of the Cumbrian retreat

The road is steep, winding and narrow
You could end up down a fell that feeds a lake
Your first mistake on Wrynose Pass
Will be the last one you ever make

Suddenly, I'm becoming more and more aware
Not making the bumps and holes set the tone
Wrynose Pass is *not* defeating me
My driving is fearless, I'm in the zone

Although it is virtually pitch black now
And other headlights are in-the-chase
This I know, yes, 100% sure
I'm in front and setting the pace

Before I know it the terrain is less severe
And tailgate headlights are almost gone
This is not the time to relax or disengage
It's just me, you see, I'm travelling alone

I turn the last bend, pull up and switch off
I now feel promoted to a new class
I step out of the car and lock the door
No victims tonight in Wrynose Pass!

Cumbria

I'm writing from Lakeland's Ambleside
This holiday is making me tired
Lots to see, lots to do
(Quite comfortable at the Hotel Vale View)
Lots more to do, lots more to see
Kodak is making a fortune from me!

Ambleside is really quite quaint
Just the resort for he who is a saint
Plenty of places to lodge and eat
And people greet you in the street
Three times I've been drawn to this base
(Something to do with the magnets in my case)

Ennerdale Water on a bright, sunny day
Can easily take your breath away
Approaching it from a high position
I saw a red arable farm engine
Near to it two little lambs were at rest
The scene was quintessentially picturesque

On the road to Buttermere the car was tossed to and fro
But on the way I felt a kind of pleasure, though
When I arrived I saw a grandeur landscape
Woods where you could get lost in and escape
Mighty mountains where you could go hunting
And views of the lake were just stunning

Next stop is the western seaport, Whitehaven
The water there was coloured blue, but now brown is given
Its marina and surrounding buildings are clean and new
The people looked happy, rested and contented too
On one of the covered piers I saw two young lovers
If only I could share this epic holiday with others

Devoke Water, the jewel in Cumbria's crown
Far away from any village or town
This is my absolute favourite tarn of all
"Gloria in excelsis Deo" I hear the angels call
Not a single man or woman in sight
Spirited away I could stay all night

And so to the deepest lake of all, Wast Water
For many it's the best; none comes after
There is a handy shop nearby this lake
Which stocks plenty of Kendal Mint Cake
Rain is not uncommon to The District
Meaning my photography here had a limit

At Ullswater on the day of my visit
I distinguished a different kind of spirit
Communication with people in the area
Was not the same as the rest of Cumbria
Got some cracking photographs from a hill
Including a passing jet aircraft until it was nil

Photography of StockGhyll woods and stream
Was in many ways a waterscape dream
The low lighting, the bridge and the waterfall
The flowing water with its rocks and all
I set up my tripod on rubble, soil and sand
And forget the clock with its flying hands

Ah, Rydal Mount, so beautiful, so handsome
William Wordsworth's home in the age of Romanticism
What wonderful words must have leaked from his quill
Poetry and prose, and whatever was his will
Dove Cottage too is where the art did flow
Walking the fells with the family in tow

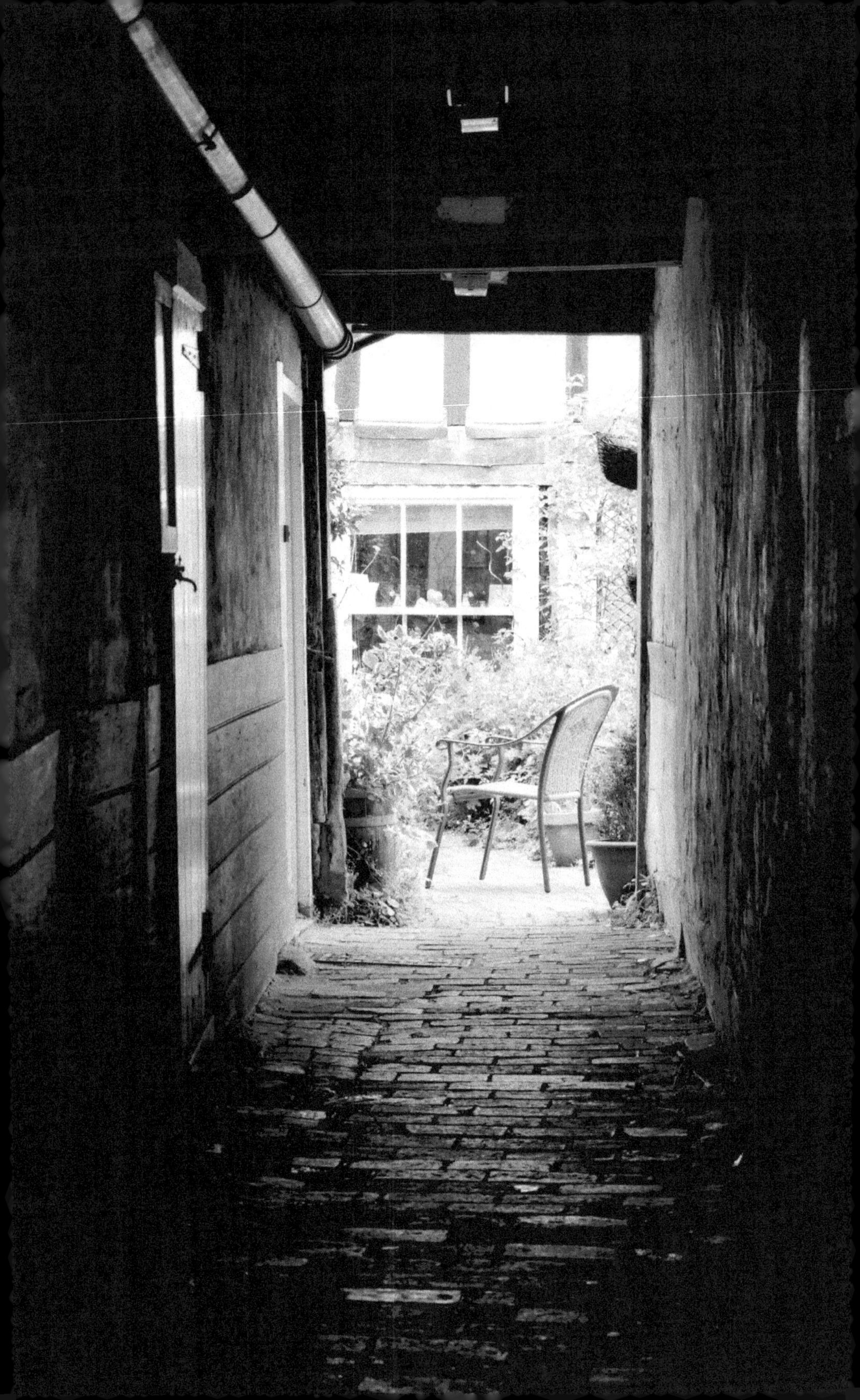

Gone Fishing

It's 3:15 am and I've just packed my lunch and kit
The predictive seaweed looks clammy as I check it
The shipping forecast confirms, rain is on the way
And hovering around minus two for most of the day

I set out for the lake, about two hours' drive
I am alone today, without my friend Clive
As I arrive it's raining and the wind has picked up
So I set my kit in place and pour my first cup

I sit back in the cold chair, chill out and wait
Will any fish like my fly today and take the bait?
My round score on the last few occasions
Has been zero, zilch, nothing to mention

But I keep coming back hoping for a bite
Day after day, and night after night
With hook, line and sinker cast in the water
Who knows, maybe today I'll catch that whopper

It's about this time I notice my cold hands and feet
So on goes the gas fire and I enjoy a little heat
When the weather is grey, wet and freezing
Just wrap up warm when you go fishing

The time now is about quarter to two
So I unwrap my sarnies and pour another brew
Only another couple of hours and I'll call it a day
And brag to Clive about the one that got away

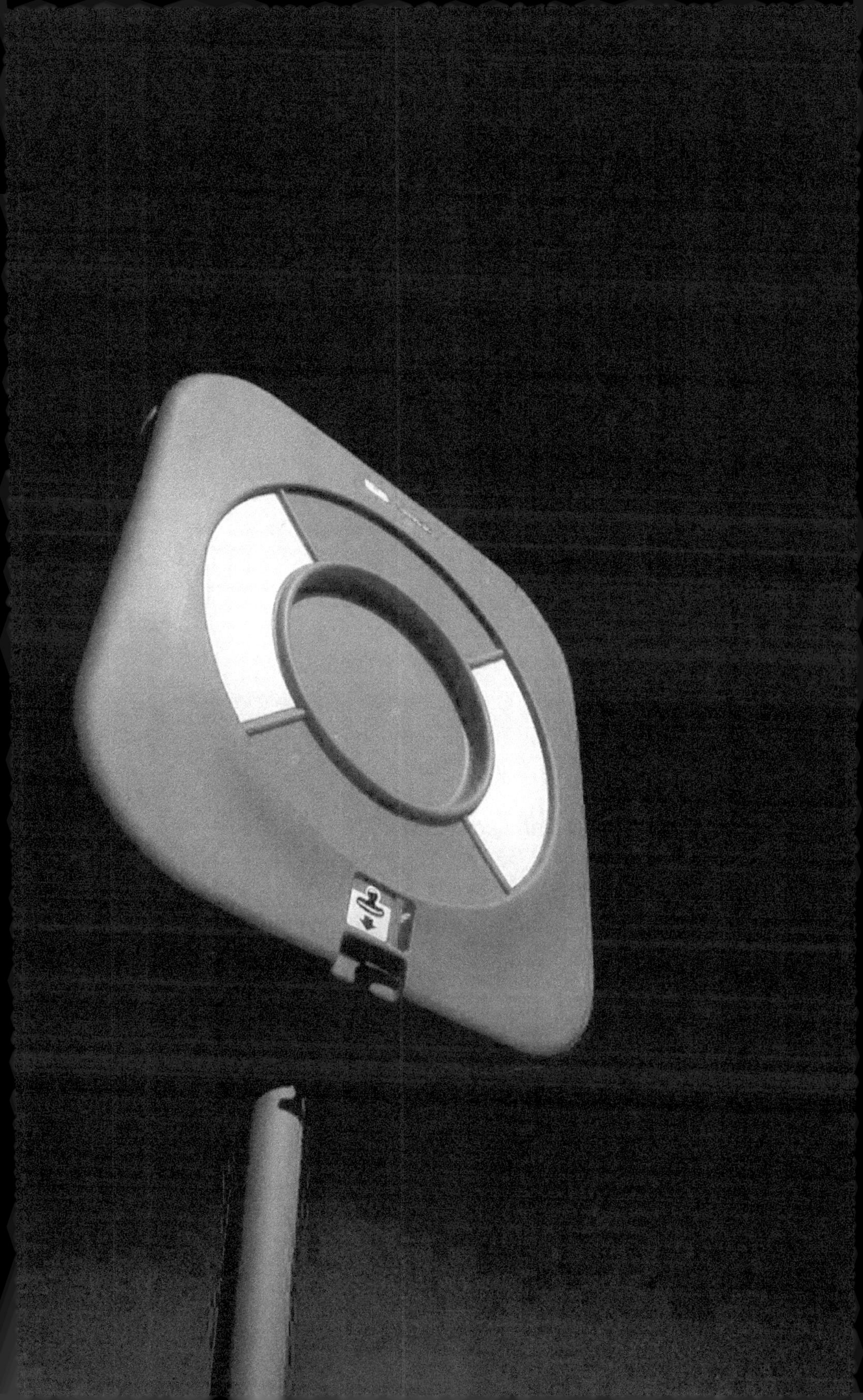

Swaying, Swaying In The Breeze

Swaying, swaying in the breeze
Dancing, dancing beneath tall tree
Moving another way in slight air
So handsome, so pretty, so fair
Hues and shades, rare and fine
What invention, what design?

Humble, humble busy bee
Buzzing, buzzing gay and free
Where next, where will he settle?
Lighting randomly on the petal
Gathering nectar as he goes
In the garden, in the meadow

Again and again the soft wind eases
Blowing, not blowing, when it pleases
Delicate flora ambles in time
Every gesture wild and sublime
Swaying, swaying in the breeze
Dancing, dancing beneath tall tree

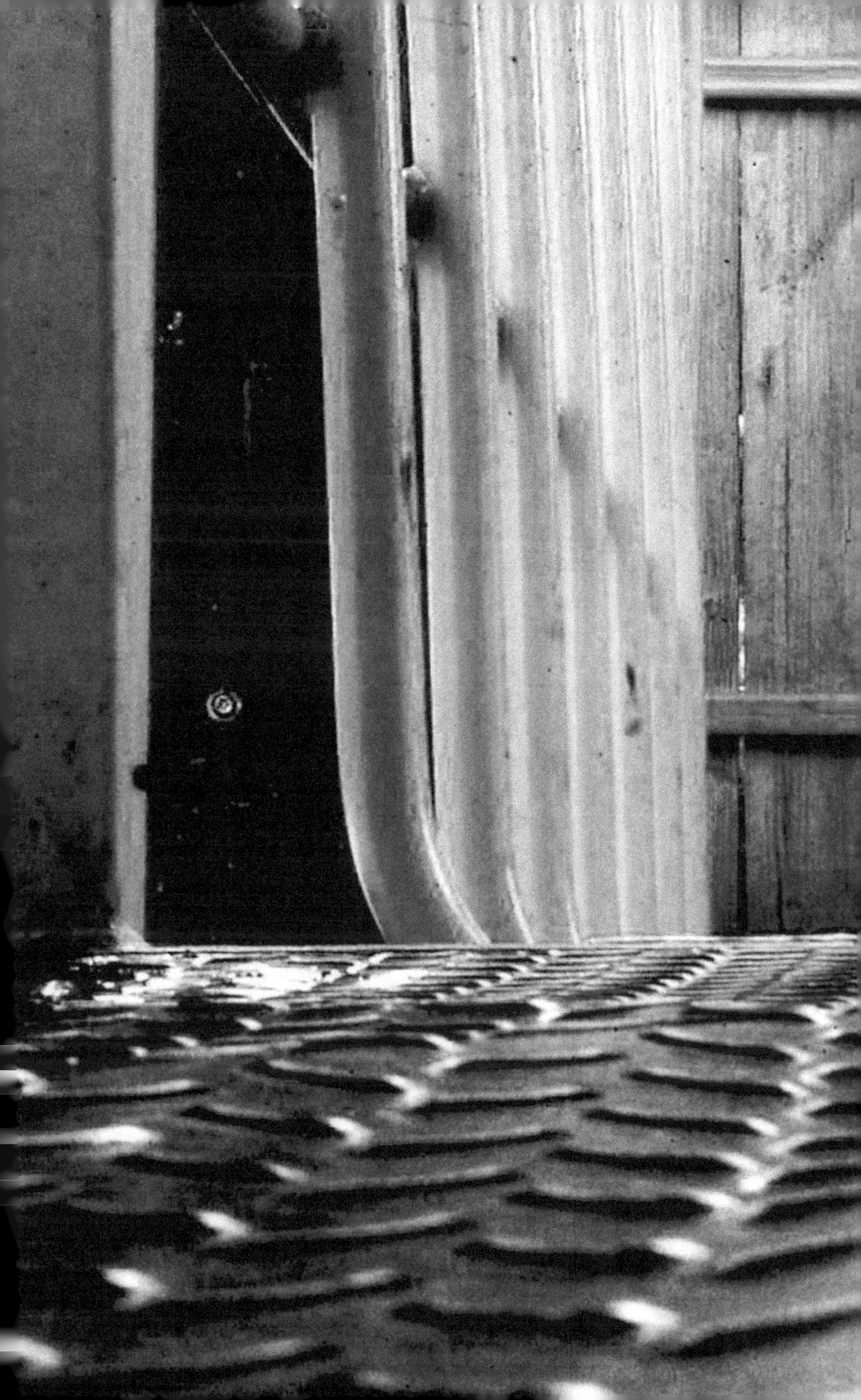

The Garden Of Eden

God created the garden of Eden
A pure unspoiled paradise
An ordered beautiful landscape
That could grow and increase in size

God placed Adam and Eve in the garden
And said, "Be fruitful and multiply
Fill the Earth and subdue it
And govern all that creep, swim and fly"

In the garden a love story began
Adam and Eve enjoying flesh-of-my-flesh
The two became an unashamed one
In the first marriage with a world to bless

Adam and Eve experienced the joy of God
His presence with them was unbroken
As strong as a three-stranded cord
That's how it was in the paradise garden

In the garden was the forbidden tree
That could cause catastrophic strife
In the midst of the garden, though
Was another tree: the tree of Life

"In the day that you eat of it you shall surely die"
God plainly said to Adam and Eve
All they had to do was not eat from the forbidden tree
Believe God, Adam and Eve, just believe!

It was the cunning, slippery serpent
That tempted Eve to sin
Adam fell too and their eyes were opened
And the cosmos became cursed as death entered in

God then drove them out of Eden
And placed the cherubim at the east
And a flaming sword that turned every way
Guarding the tree of Life and its feast

However, this is not how it all ends
We will not return to the lost Eden
Redemption and Consummation is coming
There's no plan for that ancient garden

In the future will be a greater garden
With the tree of Life on both sides of the river
Its leaves are for the healing of the nations
And the juicy, sweet fruit we will savour

Yes, we will eat from the tree of Life
Its branches regularly fully laden
Yielding a new crop every month
In the new and everlasting Eden

This Is The Month — Eastertide

This is the month
When they say that it rains and pours
Down come the showers
from heaven's open doors

But in-between the cascades
There are beams of sunlight
Shining through clouds
heavy laden and fluffy white

This is the month
When the daylight grows longer and longer
With the sun rising earlier
and setting later and later

There is also a change
In the quality of light visible in the atmosphere
This phenomenon only happens once
in the Northern Hemisphere

This is the month
When spring is well and truly here
It's time for leaping of the lamb
and the young deer

Buds are prising open
Seeds and bulbs germinate
O, the splendour
of nature's natural nascency about this date

This is the month
That brings high tides to our shores
As the moon orbits closer
and waxes more and more

These signs are where
The Jewish people take their Passover
And from where Christians
take the major holiday called Easter

There is nothing like Eastertide
Celebrating a fantastic event
It happened 2000 years ago
and I, in a sense, was present

The most spectacular display
Of God's agape love
Crucifixion and Resurrection
The only plan from above

On a Friday God laid sin on His Son
The sin of men nailed to a cross
He crucified the sinless Lamb
and took away our dross

On a Sunday Christ is raised
And we are raised with Him
This same Resurrection Power
— The Spirit — is at work within

And now we can live righteously
The old has gone, the new has come
Spreading the Good News Gospel
of what Jesus Christ has done

My Peace

Before my eyes open in the morning
At the instance of emerging from sleep
Even before I am aware of anything external
I experience something so powerful and so deep

My eyelids slowly open from their rest
And I extend one arm to test the air
Whatever my sense of touch detects
My internal peace is always there

It's the start of a brand-new day
I rise and prepare for its future
Knowing this peace will not be fazed
Because it is an inexhaustible treasure

To try and explain its presence in me
Would be like trying to describe the indescribable
You have to be inside my skin to know
And that would be impossible

This peace is from God and it guards me
Jesus left it here 2000 years ago
The first to have it were the Disciples
A special gift which you can know

Sometimes you can see it in my eyes
Or hear it behind my voice
It has something of eternal life in it
And inwardly I choose to rejoice

All pain is denied at the door
Situations and circumstances cannot penetrate
Man tries but cannot touch this core
Peace is always early and never late

When the day turns into history
And I retire in the evening in peace
I rest sweetly on my cosy pillow
And withdraw my arm back under the sheets

I gently close my eyes and rest
And before long I'm fast asleep
God has been faithful today
His gift of peace is mine to keep

This heavenly gift I received was free
And you can have it with ease
Give Jesus Christ your entire life
In return He'll give you eternal peace

The Ultimate Renewed Environment

At the end of time
When the new order has begun
And everything as we know it
has been changed in the twinkling of an eye

And the elements have been burned up
Incinerated in a pure, cleansing fire
And after the great conflagration
the cosmos that is left will be perfect

I will dance on streets of transparent gold
Bathe in a crystal river that's full of joy
Eat new fruit from a new special tree
And see with light, not from the sun, but The Son

The gravity inherent in nature and matter
will be controlled at one's own will
Even infinity will be multiplied by itself
And we will explore, and explore, and explore

No longer will we recycle
No longer will we reuse
No longer will we conserve
No longer will we repair

And this will be for longer
than anyone can calculate or imagine

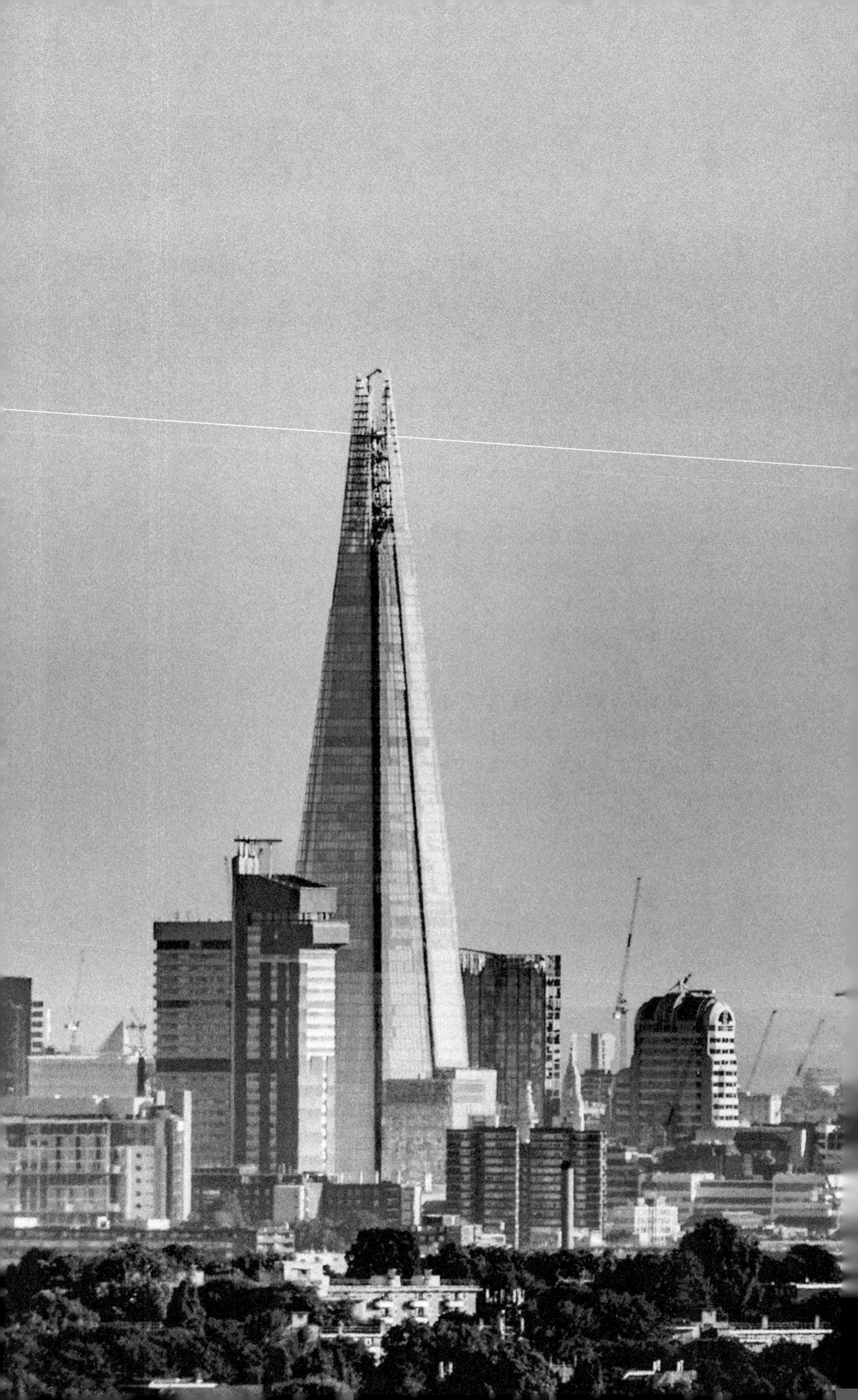

A Natural Virtuoso!

Just a few words I've penned over tea
That I hope will warm your heart and bless
Who in all the wide world could it be?
An appreciative music lover no less

Keep on practising the art and playing
Scales, broken chords and the arpeggio
And soon the classical fraternity will be saying
"She is, without doubt, a natural virtuoso!"

Her recordings are transcendent and evocative
The CDs in your hi-fi will transform your day
Listen to the exquisiteness from octave to octave
Gently close your eyes and be carried far away

In her playing are ravishing, splendid moments
Her touch cannot be in any way surpassed
Every bar conveys consistent commitment
The notes she floats in your ears will last

Her filigree technique is flawless
The critics say, "100% panache!"
The interpretations are understated yet fresh
Crescendos have plenty of style and dash

Her concert hall performances causes stomping
She charms the keyboard with unfailing eloquence
Box offices are sold out within hours of opening
The experience is worth more than pounds and pence

Her lasting impression you cannot erase
Whatever the chosen style or enharmonic keys
Stay and linger on every dripping phrase
Oh, the aural delight as she caresses the keys

Unforgettable is the rarefied pianistic alchemy
I'm captivated by this musical don
Aficionados far and wide all plea
"If music stirs the hearts of gods, play on"

The Known Great Composer

The window blinds close
The stage lights are adjusted
Two musicians walk on stage
and we welcome them warmly

As the music begins, I am transported
Transported back to the 18th century
My mind's eye can see the drying ink
on the manuscript; the autograph score

As the composer reaches the last bar
he reclines back into the chair
Instinctively he knows how it will be received
by all who hear his music

The first piece from the first composer
is in the bright and sunny C Major
Just the key to set the concert's tone
Baroque music is almost invariably effervescent

The recorder is soft and animated
And my ears cannot see the player
And the notes cause my mind to dance
and play in the thin spring air

The theorbo, just like the recorder
never draws attention to the musician
And it seems that the instrument itself
is reading the score and playing unaided

When either instrument plays solo
they both outshine their spotlight
The sound world they live in
is reborn on every musical phrase

And so to the highlight of the concert
The sonata from the great composer
Over one thousand pieces composed
Yet each imbued with unique character

Before the sonata was played
no announcement was made
And when the sonata had ended
nobody spoke the composer's name

The musicians naturally started the sonata
And they knew the audience would know
The only ones who knew the composer's name
were the musicians and the audience

Three hundred years ago music was floated
and captured by twenty-first century ears
The only people to experience this
were in the Elgar Room at the Royal Albert Hall

The JOH. SEB. BACH Limericks

J. S. Bach's Church Cantata oeuvre
Is really quite pious and pure
The melodies are holy
And so are the harmonies
For 3 liturgical calendars not 4

J. S. Bach's compositions are really intricate
The mind just boggles at the thought of it
He'll think it quite rude
If you cannot write a fugue
Especially if not in quodlibet!

Thumbs up for the Goldberg Variations
On a single manual needs explanations
It cures insomnia
Like no other
Just follow the instructed articulations

J. S. Bach's compositions for cello
Especially the ones that are solo
If played in rubato time
You'll find them quite fine
And positively smooth and mellow

Ludwig van Beethoven

Listen to the Kreutzer Sonata
Unmistakable are his 9 symphonies
Diabelli Variations are the finest
Without hearing for much of his life
Inexcusable if played without passion
Glorious how he resolves each composition

Varied are the 32 piano sonatas
Achieving transcendence like no other
New Testament repertoire they are dubbed

Bagatelles are brisk and bright
Energising are the piano concertos
Engrossing is the Missa Solemnis
Trio for the Archduke Rudolph of Austria
Heart-wrenching Romance No. 2
Opus 20 Septet is full of tunes
Virtuosic Violin Concerto in D Major
Entertaining Choral Fantasia in C minor
Nothing like the groundbreaking string quartets

"O Love As Long As You Can!"

O come you anticipated day
The one to have live music fall upon the ear
Come quickly and do not delay
But wait I must
And wait I will...

Days went by and I waited
The morning of the concert I waited
On the way to the concert I waited
Minutes before the concert I waited

The piano was open and it waited
The air was hushed – even it waited

And now, at last, the waiting was over
The time for the audience to wait was over

It's time
And the soprano floats into view
She enters gracefully and with ease
And the audience welcomes both her
And the pianist in their stage right

The concert begins and each song tells a story
Causing a cloud filled sky to be cloudless again
And shining sunlight through the windows of the Chamber
All brought about by the energy in the music

And then it happened
My attention was seized
By Liszt's first notes
Of a lyrical song

Piano introduced
Captivating melody
Effortlessly flowing
Hungarian confectionery

"O lieb so lang du lieben kannst!"
("O love as long as you can!")
These first few words were exclaimed
Then more of the liebestraum followed

Sixteen lines of overflowing overflow
Heights and depths, refined and raw
Sweet and soft, and roaring roars

And then
This song comes to an end
And I plummet from the stratosphere
Emerge from the deep sea dive
Take my first breath and think
"So that's what it's like to breathe"

Consciously I breathe
And breathe again and again
I keep on breathing until it becomes unconscious

I wipe the non-existent tear from my face
Because it still remains in the corner of my eye

Other lieder come and go
Yes, they must
The concert must finish
Time must start working again...

My Well-Tempered Broadwood

My well-tempered Broadwood
Has a sound like no other
The first time I played her
I was besotted by the tones

Other pianos tried their best
To woo and charm my ears
Some were just run-of-the-mill
Others pale, common or unfortunate

Other pianos looked shiny new
Their appearance and design first class
They had utmost physical prowess
That was very attractive and smart

It was the Scherzo in D Major
From Beethoven's Pastorale Sonata
That caused me to internally shout, "wow!"
I have never heard these chords like this — ever!

In all my listening of the radio
I had never heard this sound
In all my CD recordings
This sound could not be found

Again I played the descending chords
And was stunned by the strings vibrations
Again and again I played the music
And knew she had to be mine

Years have come and gone
And still the musical affair continues
Nothing has ever edged close
To the sound of my beloved Broadwood

If ever there was truth in music
Then maybe, just maybe, this could be it
Consistent, reliable, joyous, distinctive
My Broadwood is the ultimate yardstick

So what other clues can I give you
To the sound my Broadwood makes
That would give you a clearer picture
Of the sound dimension where it exists

Early music in the Classical era
Is where I feel it sits
From Haydn to Mozart to Beethoven
These were the first greats with plaudits

Chopin and Liszt are also noted
To have moved across the ebony and ivory
Playing and composing rapturous harmonies
On the Broadwood's 88 black and white

John Broadwood & Sons also happens to be
The maker of pianos for Queen Elizabeth II
The Royal Warrant it owns and adorns
Is the longest in British history

One final thought I'll leave with you
Did Beethoven 'hear' the 'same' Scherzo
That made my ears fall hopelessly in love
Even though he was deaf as a dodo?

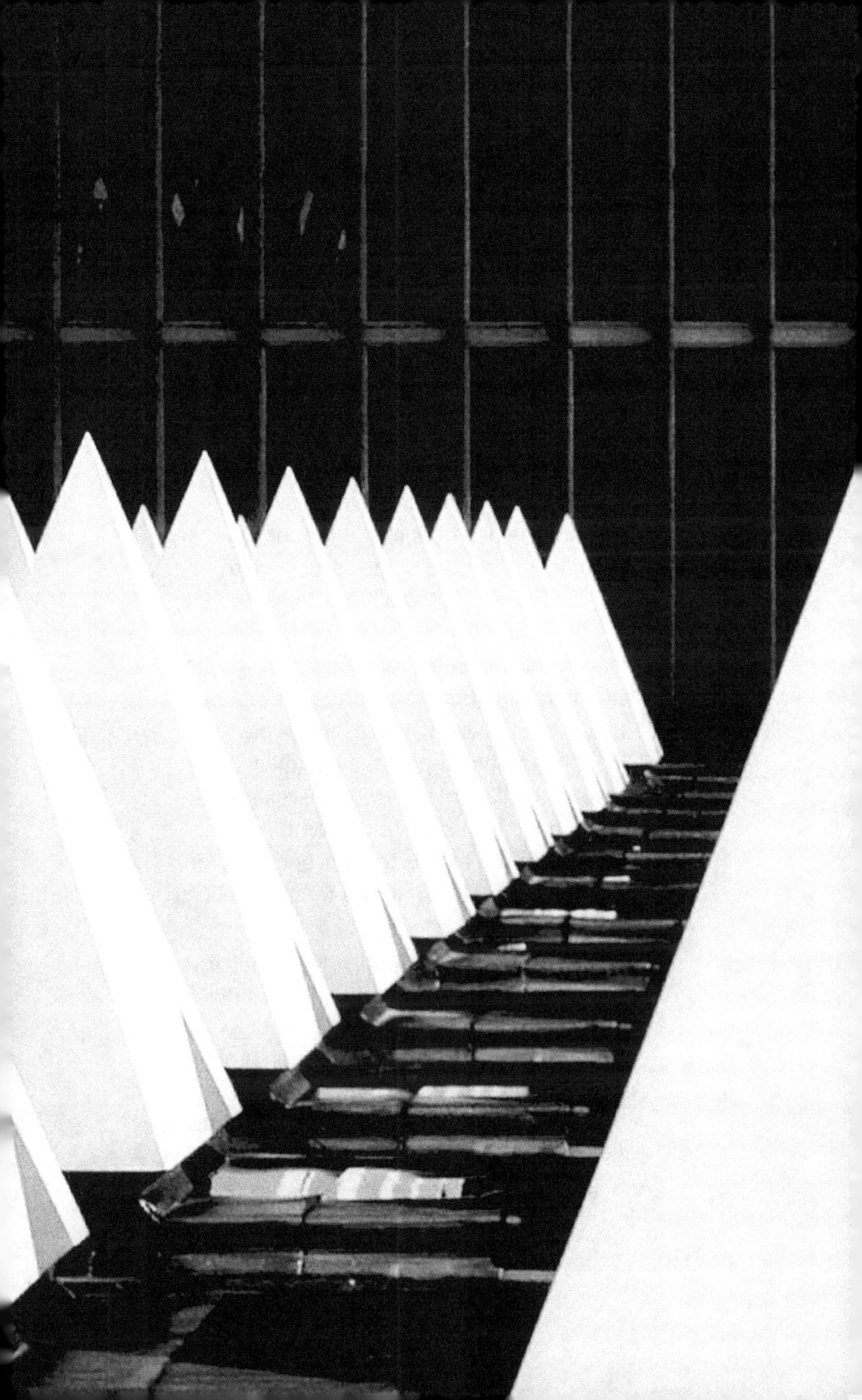

Avril's New Car

When winter sets in or comes the rain
Must she rely on bus or train?
Or could total independence be her aim?
Whatever the reason, whatever the vein
She had decided, "never again!"
For horses she has bought without their manes
Some call it a car, some call it a wain
Cause SAAB Automobile is its name

As she speeds down the road on the inside lane
With the metal horses she struggles to tame
She almost takes off like a jet aeroplane!
And I hear her friends repeat the heightened refrain
"Look out, it's that supersonic Avril again
A petrol head with high octane on the brain!"
Using her skill she avoids the bus and the crane
With a handbreak turn that is far from plain

Then one day her car begins to complain
A flat battery, worn clutch — oh what a pain!
And escalating running costs she cannot explain
On her pocket this is an unforeseen drain
Whatever the hardship, whatever the strain
Avril's enthusiasm does not dwindle or wane
The love for her car is absolute and it shall remain
And so shall the queen of the highways reign!

Mr Spock And The Lost Left Sock

Fiddily, fiddily Mr Spock
Up and down the road he ran
Looking for his lost left sock
Knitted by his dear old nan

It has tassels and conker size knots
Is a bit smelly and very, very old
It is green with pink and yellow spots
And ventilation holes, so I'm told

Could Captain Kirk have hidden it?
Or Scotty used it to gain warp factor speed?
Or Bones made it into liquid chemicals
To inject into the Klingon's spleen?

"I've found it, I've found it!"
Comes Mr Spock's cry
"Lieutenant Uhura has used it
To make cheese and onion pie"

Mr Spock's belly rumbles
As he spies the culinary delight
But Chekov quickly snatches it
And tucks in with 3 or 4 bites

Mr Spock is speechless
And finds it hard to believe
So he puts his thumb into his mouth
And sobs on Zulu's sleeve

Just another day on the Starship Second Prize
Tomorrow's episode promises more
As they continue on their great commission:
"To boldly eat more cheese and onion pies than before!"

Billy-Nilly

Billy-Nilly
Was quite silly
He hadn't got a clue!
He put ice cream in his carne
to make it more runny
This story is absolutely true

Then brushes his teeth
With a fresh rhubarb leaf
Don't try this at home
Gargles with puréed garlic
then feels quite sick
So goes to bed all alone

Billy-Nilly
Was quite silly
He hadn't got a clue!
He put mānuka honey
on fried Spanish salami
This story is absolutely true

He likes jalapeño chili
With his cream, fruit and jelly
And sardines smothered in Marmite
Horseradish in porridge
Lemon curd and sage
Washed down with turmeric and sprite

His cuisine repertoire
Is not really bizarre
Everyone likes blancmange with chips
And noodles in grilled gâteau
Curried cornflakes cooked slow
Eased down with paraffin from ships

Billy-Nilly
Was quite silly
He hadn't got a clue!
He goes to the shop
on a one leg hop
This story is absolutely true

He buys fresh air
From rural Zaire
Paying far, far too much
It's an acquired delicacy
enjoyed by his pet flea...
Oh yes, and also the Dutch

He buys fresh Olympic flame
And puts it in a paper frame
Then wonders why his house burns down
Oh well, just one of those things
He'll move in with his pet goslings
And cry big tears like a clown

Then thinks he oughta
Buy red Martian water
And put some in his car's engine
Some he will drip
on his bottom lip
And dilute the rest one part to 10 million

Billy-Nilly
Was quite silly
He closes his eyes when rounding a bend
Does not like the future
But loves an adventure
What's better is watching goldfish no end!

His favourite hobby
Is painting the lobby
At least three times a week
He's been through every shade
From brilliant white to black spade
Vibrant colours, he says, are too weak

Conversations with him
Are like going to the gym
After two minutes you're exhausted
But when you look in the mirror
your biceps are bigger
And you are absolutely flabbergasted

There's no one like Billy-Nilly
Except on the Isles of Scilly
I think it's something to do with the grass
Everyone there
never stands and stares
They just tip their hats when they pass

Billy-Nilly can work out every logarithm
And knows Shakespeare's entire compendium
That's just two for a start
Another two would be
entries in The Grove Dictionary
And the complete neuroscience of the heart

Not many people know
That when he plays the piano
He throws the rule book out the window
He starts at the last bar
playing backwards with a, "ah, ha, haa!"
Not missing a single pianissimo or fortissimo!

As you can see
Balmy Billy-Nilly
Is really having a lot of fun
Whatever you may thinks
You and your copious links
He does it all to the audience of One

High Street!

(Outside In – Inside Out)

Why is that single launderette chair in the middle of the road?
And the writing inside all wrong – it's all back-to-front!
The people who wrote those words and printed them
Can't write or spell a thing – no they just can't!

Those three storey buildings where people live and work
Look so small behind the serifed lettered window
The wall-mounted lampshade is just as large as one floor
Everything looks different from what I used to know

These houses fit nicely in the centre of that door mat
The numbers above one window are just like a four berth tent
And reads one penny short of twenty-five pounds
With an annual percentage rate of zero percent

People in this land are shockingly backward
Almost every single letter reads from right to left
They hang enormous clothes on motorbikes and cars
And hop on indoor buses that are not frequent

On every street junction in the middle of the road
They play darts, drink tea and eat currant buns
Whilst sitting on chintz covered chairs at Bauhaus tables
And wave at whizzing juggernauts just for fun

The people here prefer to drive their cars inside
Even the road signs are inside on all but the ground floors
As for the trees, well, they just copy the cars and the road signs
And grow quite healthily in the spacious sunny indoors

Then a car made of natural shimmering, streaky, speed blur
Drives straight through a glass partition and parks under a plant
What's so amazing about this is that the glass doesn't even break
Then flips over and points to the sky at an 80 degrees slant

Look, there are more gigantic second-hand woolly jumpers
They seem to prefer gathering in sunny alfresco scenes
Just hanging there on their hangers in the middle of the street
And the cars won't pass until they change from red to green

I really must replace these glasses with the polarised variety
Seeing everything as half reversed and translucent is quite bizarre
When I take them off this land is more ludicrously bewildering
Then again, I'll keep them on and apply dollops of sauce tartare

At last, I've come to a civilised and sensible office space
Although, it's situated right in the middle of the street
I can see desks, office chairs, a photocopier, office forms
And charging elephants, wild horses, a cockatoo and a parakeet

In one Union-Jacked chippy was a spotless, silver serving counter
Behind it stood a very short man in two-dimensional profile
His head was the size of an overinflated beach ball
His hair was of reversed letters, but he had a lovely smile

And, even more extraordinary: a reflection reflecting itself
Now everything keeps reversing and turn, turning about
Spiegel Im Spiegel melodies go round inside my head
On and on and on it goes; outside in, inside out

Can this land get any curiouser and curiouser, Alice?
Rabbit holes certainly look different from the top
I'll examine reflections from a different perspective
By looking through them from the inside of shops

Coffee shops are decidedly best for this activity
I'll take a pew and choose espresso — no sugar
And a large slice of crème crowned caffè latte cake
Then soon I'll emerge from my diurnal slumber

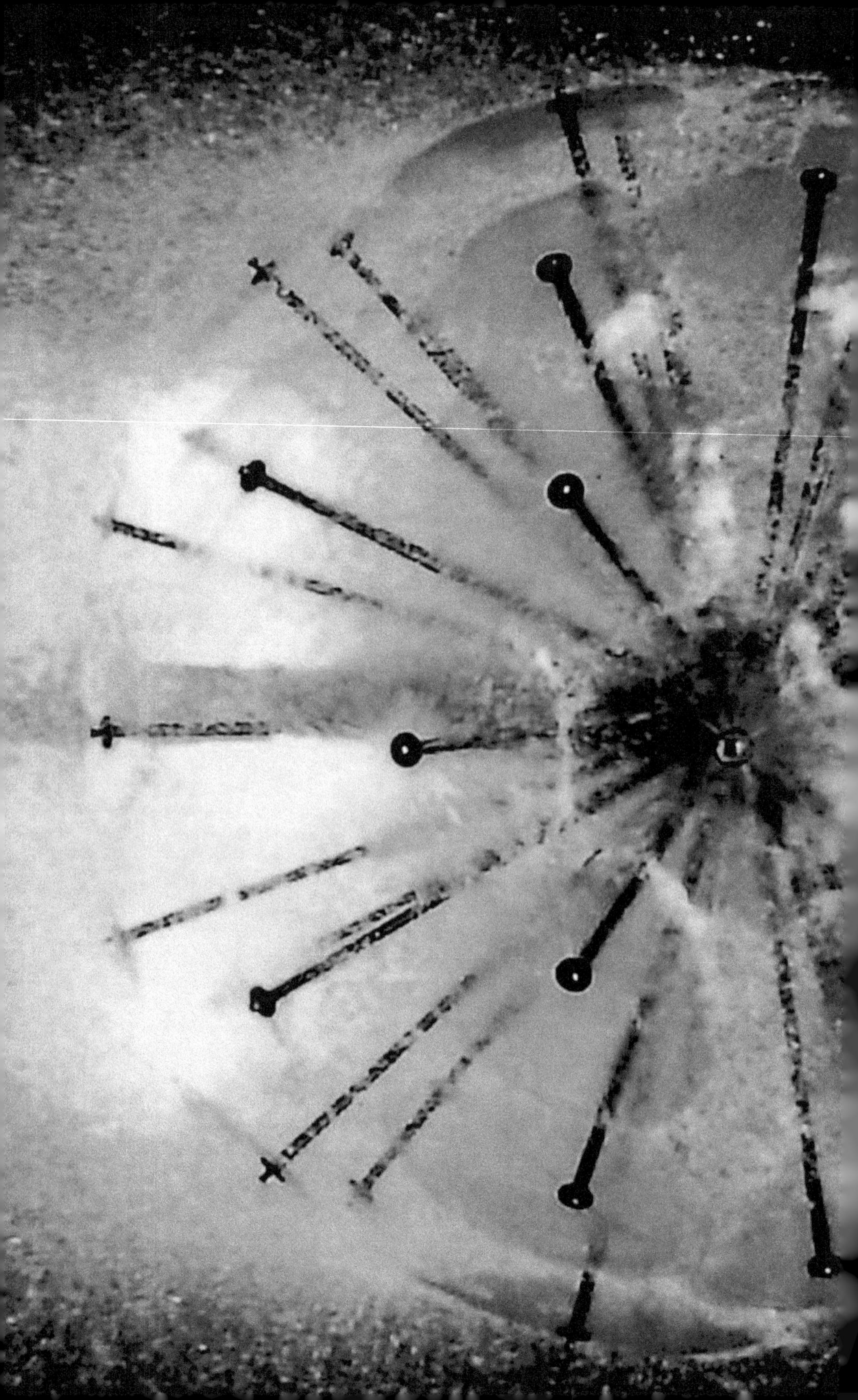

Saffron And Wine Lamb

Hovering over a gastronaut
And playing with his thought
Is where you will find this dish

It brings excitement to the palate
Then straight down the gullet
And his stomach says, "delish!"

It serves two that are hungry
Or even up to three
This recipe is complete

Enjoyed by the refined
With suitable red wine
It's a real gourmet treat

Saffron is key with the wine and the lamb
Add fresh onions and garlic by hand
And also a few sprigs of rosemary

Roasted new potatoes
And shredded cavolo nero
Are the chosen complementaries

A special cuisine to savour
With a fine, delicate flavour
Just perfect for that occasion

Guaranteed to satisfy
Why not give it a try?
An absolute taste revelation!

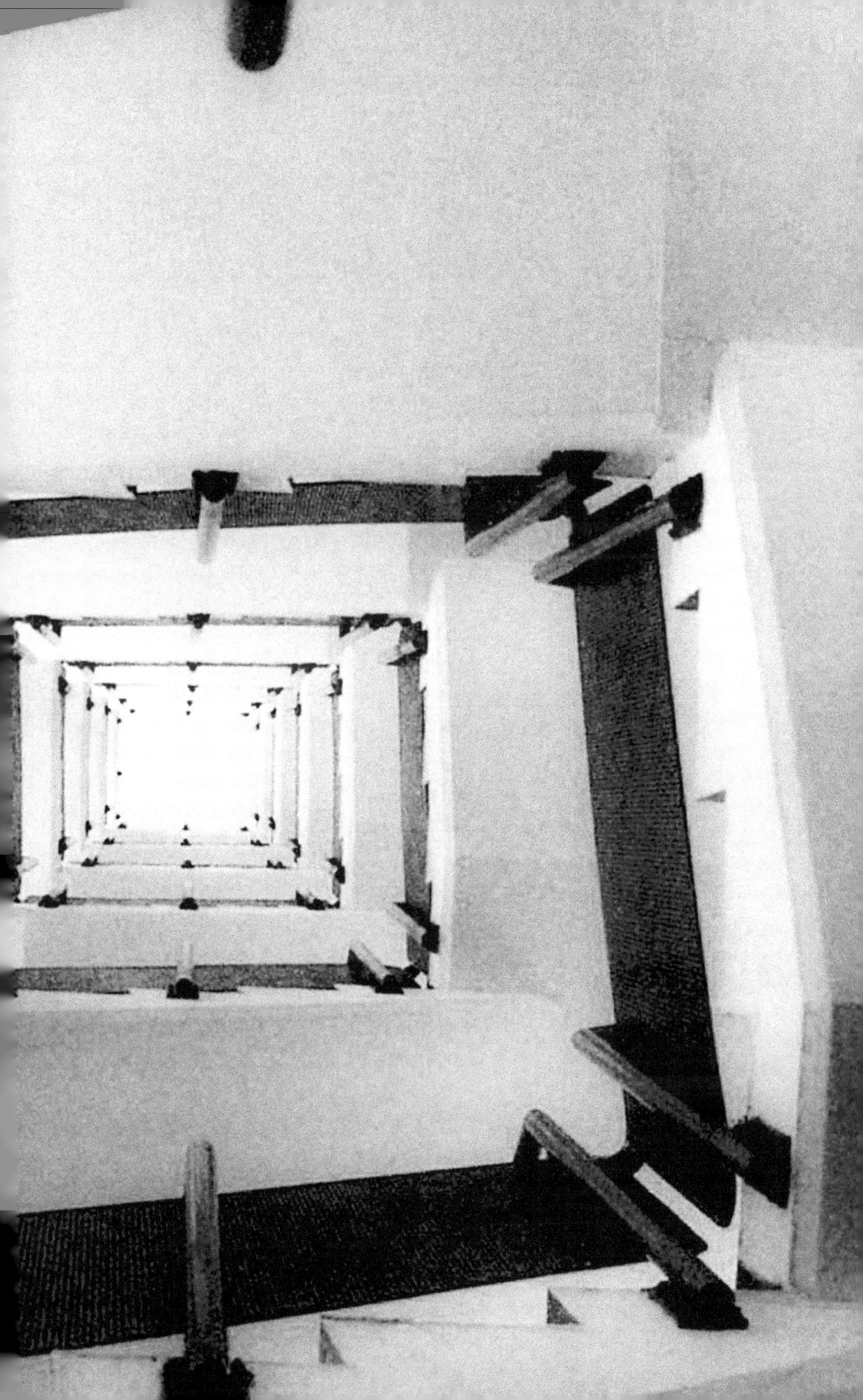

Dear Maiden, Fair Maiden

Dear Maiden
Fair Maiden
As sweet as a ripened pear

Dear Maiden
Fair Maiden
With miles and tons of flair

Dear Maiden
Fair Maiden
Whose presence charms the air

Dear Maiden
Fair Maiden
Whose finery is common ware

Dear Maiden
Fair Maiden
With rich flowing hair

Dear Maiden
Fair Maiden
With eyes crystal clear

Dear Maiden
Fair Maiden
Whose likeness is quite rare

Dear Maiden
Fair maiden
Cosmopolitan, compassionate and cares

Dear Maiden
Fair Maiden
Who soothes the tragic king Lear

Dear Maiden
Fair Maiden
Troubadours play faint everywhere

Dear Maiden
Fair Maiden
Whose beauty brings a tear

Dear Maiden
Fair Maiden
Silences the gloomy soothsayer

Dear Maiden
Fair Maiden
As fresh as the New Year

Dear Maiden
Fair Maiden
To my heart is very near

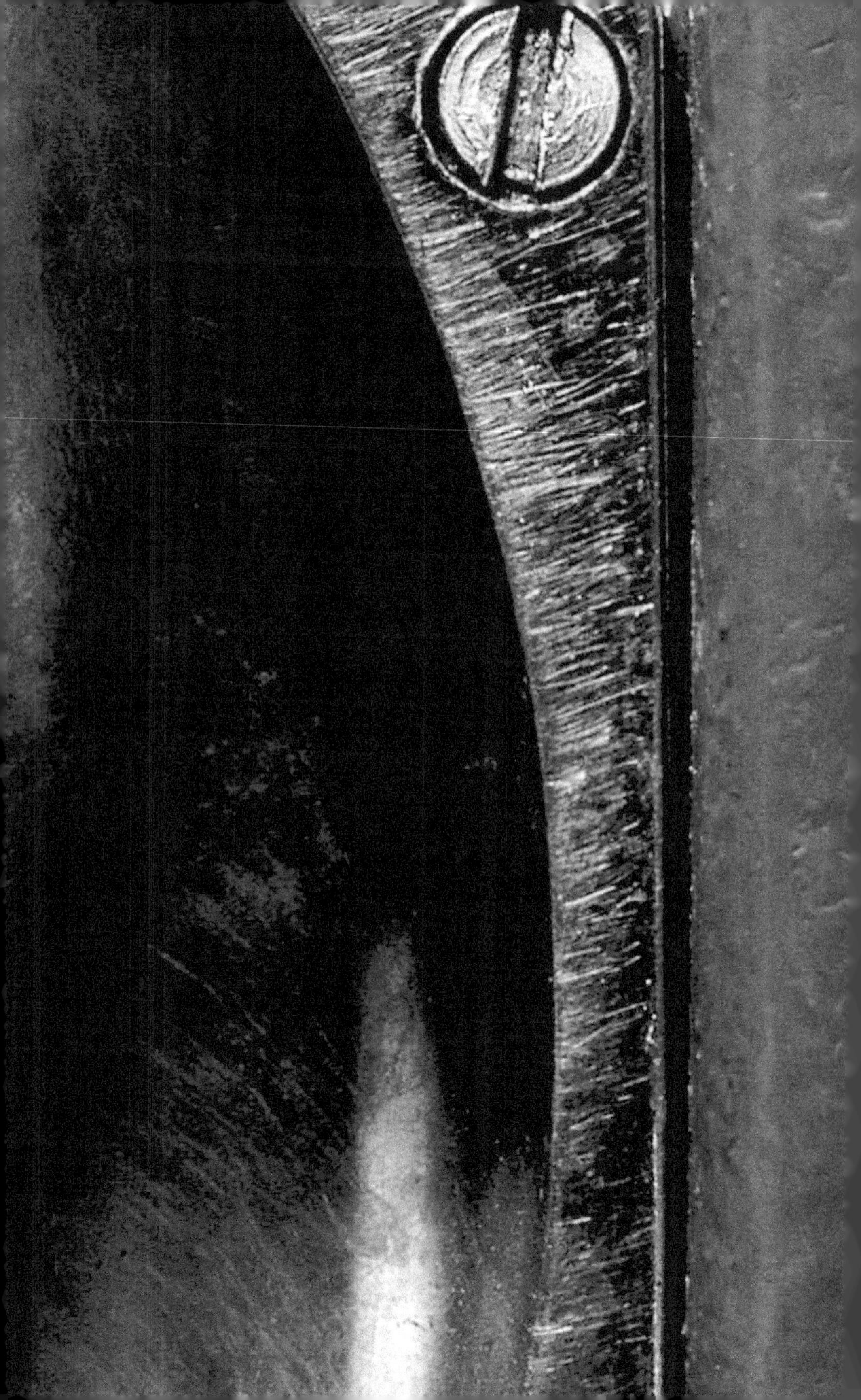

Pair Extraordinaire!

Happy, happy days to you both
Since before you were betrothed
Exquisite and rare bonbons
Such are this Patrick and Yvonne

Opening their hearts and home
Their lives read like a palindrome
So glad they won't ever stad
From being godly mum and dad

Gifted and talented children
Sharing their genes from within
Special and dear are their friends
And their love for them never ends

When they look into each other's eyes
One's mind can only espy
A youthfulness in their glance
From first mutual love in France

With a love that has no cure
And a future that is secure
Excited at what it holds
When their grandchildren are old

Where Would The Summer Be...?

Where would the summer be
If it wasn't for Nemone
Born on the 22nd of June, actually!

Sing the songs you love to sing
The one that the angels bring
Far better than the nightingale's offering

Write a masterpiece, write at will
Write from the heart, mind and soul until
Shakespeare has to lay down his quill

Dance until you're out of breath
Dance when there is nothing left
Dance as Fonteyn with Nureyev

God has given you gifts and not by chance
So pursue them in the way of excellence
Both here and in the favourite land of France

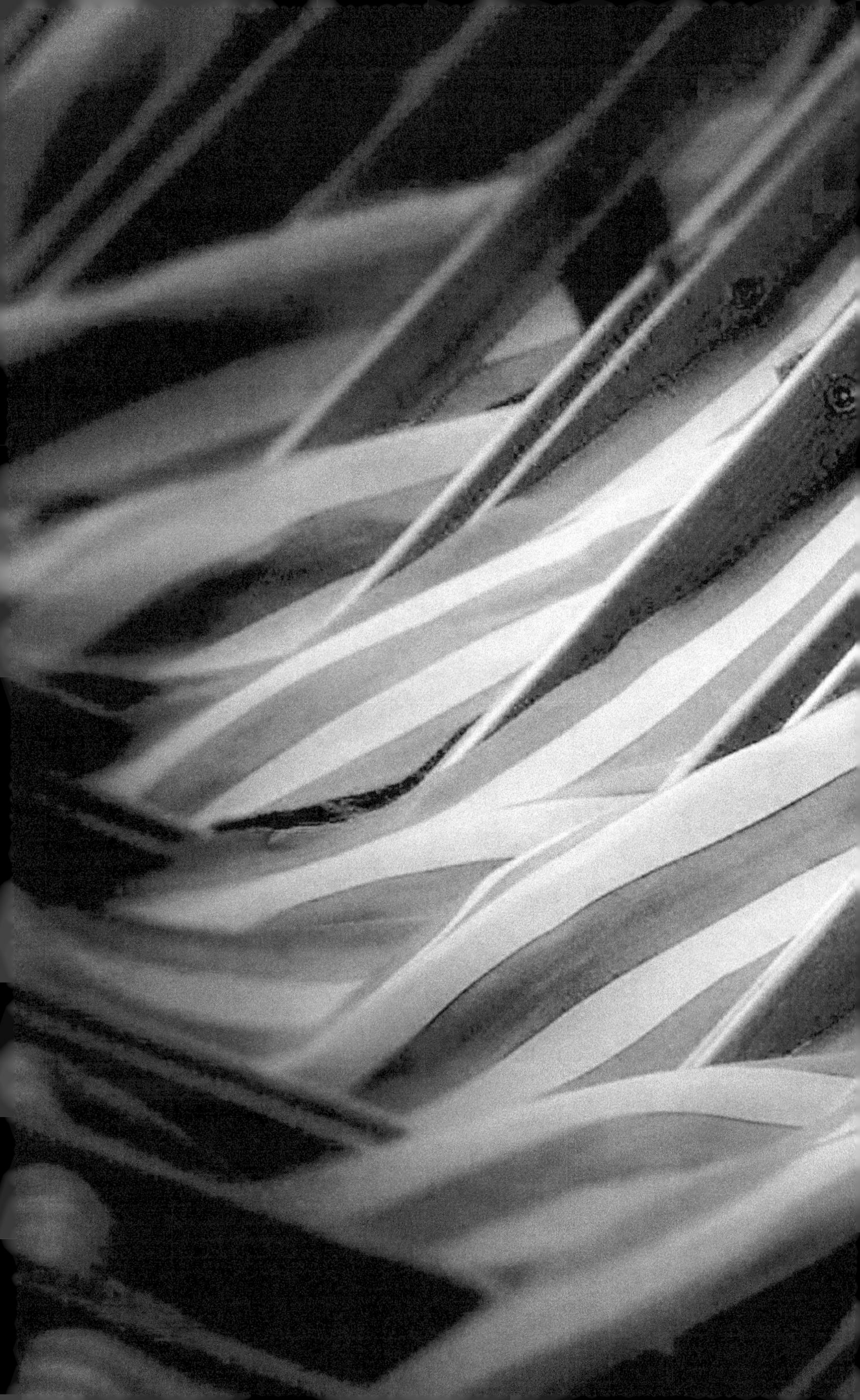

"The Greeting Kiss"

The greeting kiss
The holy kiss
Never to miss
This welcome kiss

Means so much
Breakfast, tea, lunch
Without a thought
And never taught

Just a touch
Then its over
Sets the tone
Light as feather

It means welcome
It means bless
It means connected
It means love

"Good, you're here"
"I know you"
"In the beloved"
Feels so true

"The kettle's on
Have a seat
Cup of tea?
Slice of cake?"

Perfect with hug
Raises a smile
Eye to eye
"Stay a while"

Just a peck
Left and right
Right and left
Italian or French

Between our friends
Between our family
Between fellow Christians
Instinctive and automatic

Suitor to suitress
Hand gently taken
Bows down head
To touch tenderly

Major key prelude
Priming the canvass
"Whatever happens next
You are loved"

Expression of endearment
From the heart
Warmth from within
Warmth outside too

"Truth and honesty
It will continue"
The first kiss
It must last

The greeting kiss
The holy kiss
Never to miss
This welcome kiss

The Parting Kiss

It is early in the morning
The best part of the day
A new, fresh canvas
to create a unique 24 hours
of our lives together

We have breakfast
Grab the car keys
and say, "See you later, darling"
as the front door is closed
But one thing you have forgotten to do

You turn around before the gate
Walk back up the garden
Open the front door
And your spouse begins
"Have you forgotten...?"

You warmly enfold one another
Look into each other's eyes and say
"I love you so much, darling"
You give each other a special kiss
Smile and continue on your journey

Both of their days will be okay, now
because of their expressed affections
Whatever happens today
there will be no accidents
And all because of that kiss

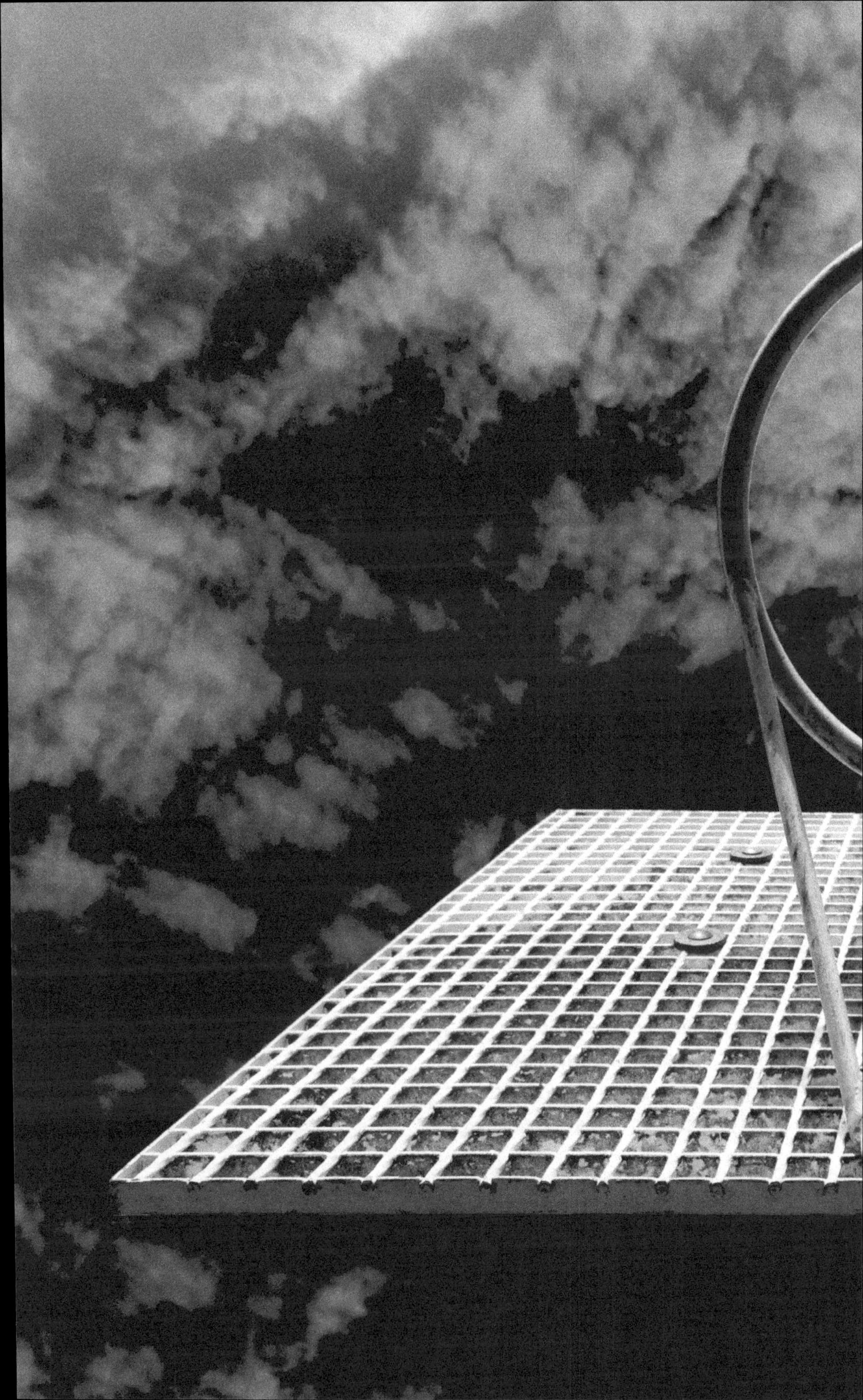

Summer Rain

A few moments ago we left the hall
where we had enjoyed the concert
It was a lunchtime concert
and finished about 2:30pm

On the programme were waltzes
polkas and arrangements of minuets
While we were there our toes tapped
and our heads swayed a bit, too

Now that the concert was over
we strolled back to the car
and decided to walk through
the ornamented landscape gardens

Midsummer's Day was last week
Melodies of high bird song was heard
And the bistro beckoned us
"Come, sample some delights"

So we took our seats near the maze
Decided iced tea and gâteau
And after placing our order
we just sat for a second or two

As we sat under the parasol
we then talked about the concert
How springlike and gai
the quartet had sounded and played

As our tea and cake arrived
there were a few light drops
beginning to fall on the parasol
Just a little passing shower?

Thud.......... thud.......... thud..........
Then the intervals grew shorter
Thud... thud... thud... thud... thud...
And the birds in the trees gradually silenced
as the sound of the rain grew

The fine, light rain was first quiet
Starting as a hushed pianissimo
But, the composer had written a crescendo

This wet summer chorus
was like the increasing sound
of a sizzling frying pan

"Can you hear it?" I said
"Nature is playing a waltz"

I stood up
Stepped out from under the parasol
and offered my right hand
And you accepted my invitation

We adopted the position:
Hand in hand
Hand on back
Hand on shoulder
An indivisible one

We started slow and in time
Thud, 2, 3... thud, 2, 3... thud, 2, 3...
But the tempo was increasing
Ziz-zl-ing, ziz-zl-ing, ziz-zl-ing

We had to keep in step
From adagio…
to andante…
to maestoso…

Our gestures becoming more defined
From pianissimo…
to mezzo piano…
to forte…

Round and round the music took us
Our expressions wider and wider
Our heart beats were synchronised
All in perfect decorum

We were caught up in the music
It swept us off our feet
I swirled you round and round
First left to right, then right to left

On the outside was a summer shower
On the inside the tempest was free
Lightning bolts electrifying our souls
Waves crashing on the beach

By now, heels and tuxedo were saturated
But we could not stop
We could not stop the dancing
until the very last drop

When the clouds broke
And the sun came out again
We heard the birds singing
And we smiled

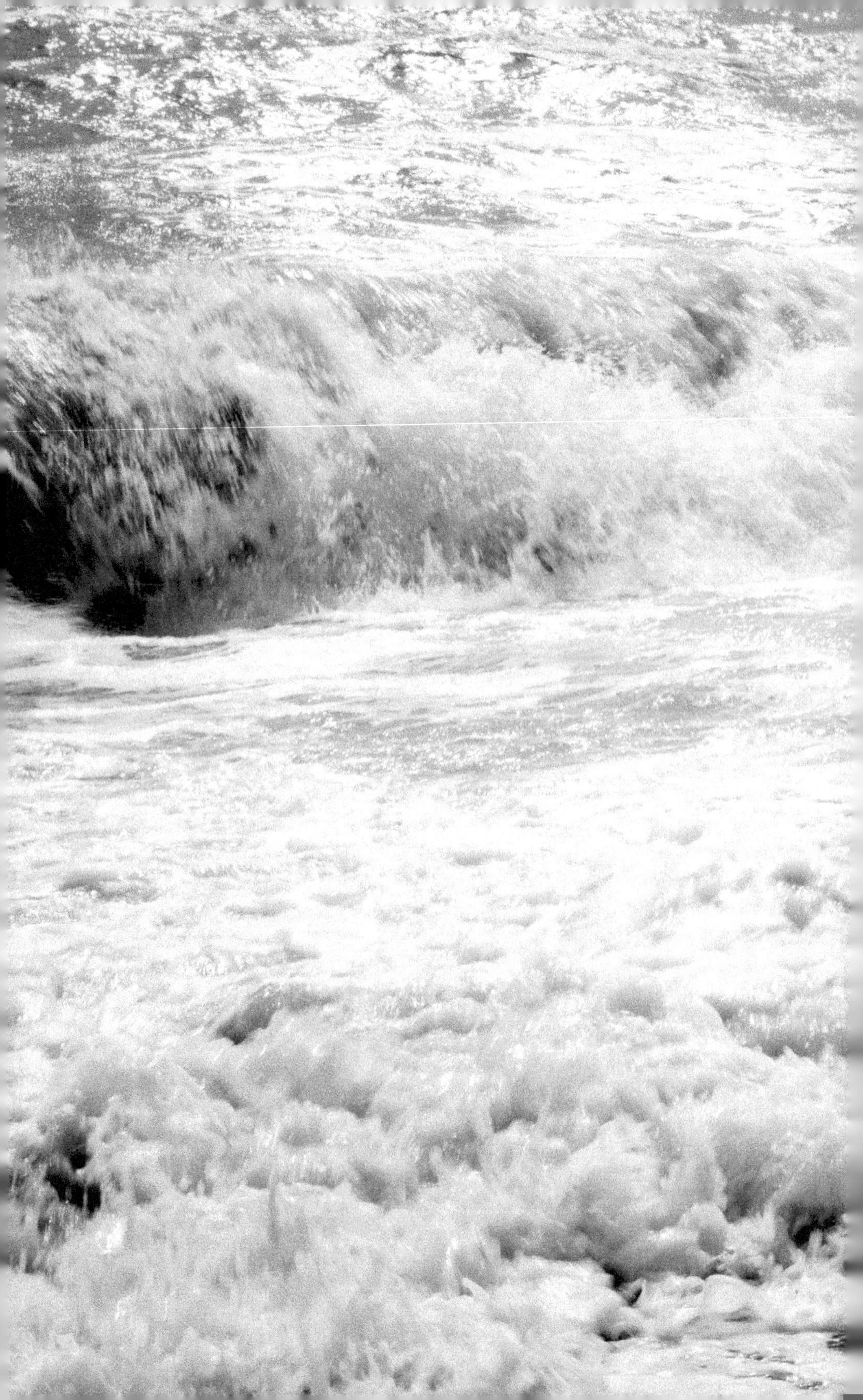

Images: Pictures In My Mind

What can you see when you look through my eyes?
The photons as they make
an upside-down impression on my retina?
The resultant charge as it passes along
my optic nerve
and into the visual cortex?
And how the excited neurons
inter-play with both
the psychology of vision
and what makes me, me?

Can you see the world as I see it?
With all I can consciously see
and the physical objects that are real
and yet I cannot consciously see?
And all that I see
and don't consciously see
affects my relation to the world?

Can you see that I see a multiplicity of love?
Agape — unconditional love
Eros — romantic love
Philia — affectionate love
Philautia — self-love
Storge — familiar love
Pragma — enduring love
Ludus — playful love
Mania — obsessive love

Can you see that I see beauty in every dimension?
But the beauty that is of the spiritual dimension
is the most beautiful of all!

Can you see that I see the radiance of the sun?
Even when it's cloudy
or at night
or when the room has no windows
the sun is still in full radiance — that's what I see

Can you see nature's wildflowers and wild animals?
They are free and controlled by no man

Can you see the words of a writer before he pens them?
The distillation process in his mind
of his life
the life of others
the immaterial life
and the life to come?

Can you see the effects of music on the listener's ear?
Not just the physics
but the physiological, too?
The melodies, the harmonies
the character of each major key
the character of each minor key
and the character of the chromatic?
All this can be evocative
as well as experiencing the future now

Can I see the pictures in your mind
as you hear my words?
Is your picture complete
or do I need to give you more paint?

Can you see the lifted countenance of someone you love?
Just imagine God's expression
— His lifted countenance —
when it is accompanied
by His sonorous tones that reverberates
"Well done good and faithful servant"

Can you see the artist as he captures?
The intentions?
The statements?
The audience?
The art?

Can you see God's work of art?
His masterpiece is you!
His masterpiece is your neighbour!
Can you see what his masterpieces will be like in the future?

Can you see the pictures in my mind?

Themed audiobook on two CDs

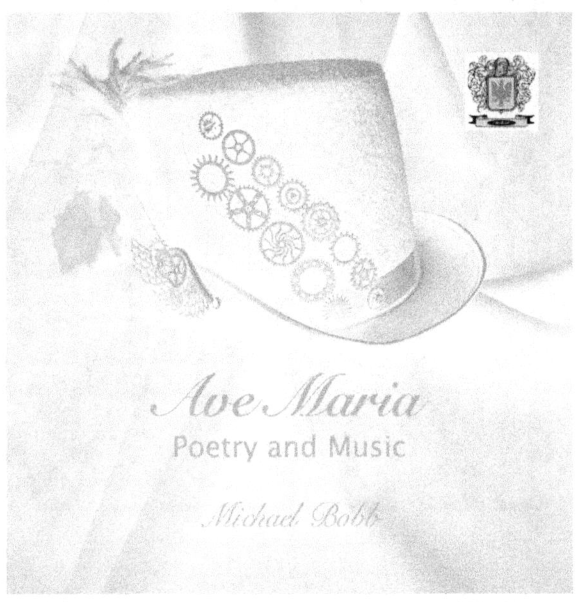

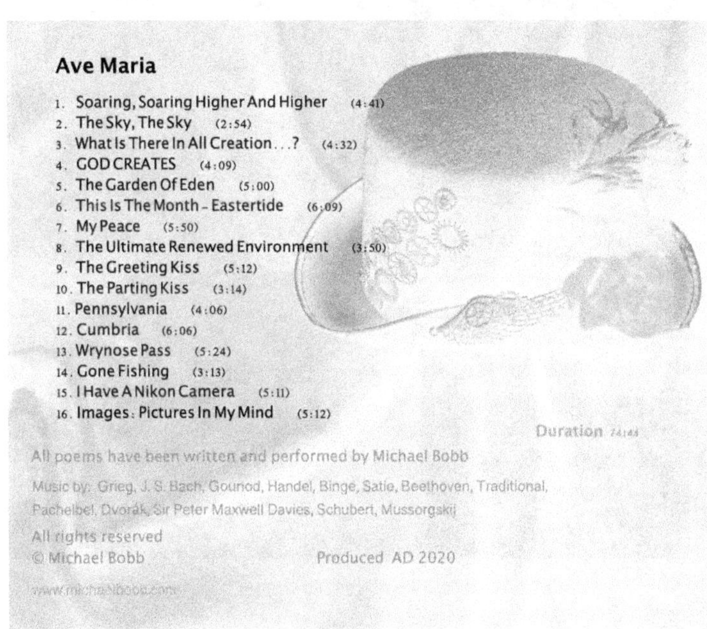

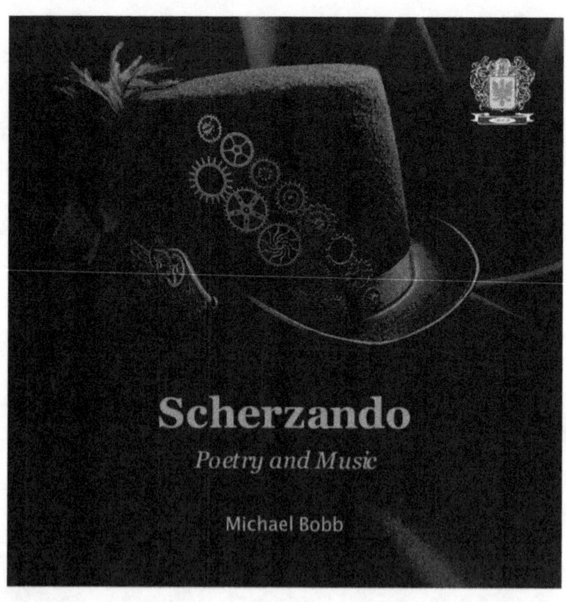

Scherzando
Poetry and Music
Michael Bobb

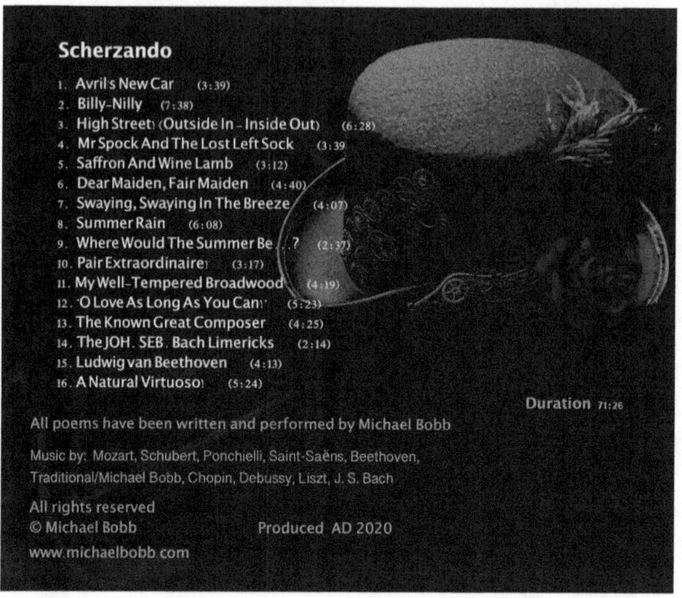

Scherzando
1. Avril's New Car   (3:39)
2. Billy-Nilly   (7:38)
3. High Street (Outside In – Inside Out)   (6:28)
4. Mr Spock And The Lost Left Sock   (3:39)
5. Saffron And Wine Lamb   (3:12)
6. Dear Maiden, Fair Maiden   (4:40)
7. Swaying, Swaying In The Breeze   (4:07)
8. Summer Rain   (6:08)
9. Where Would The Summer Be   ?   (2:37)
10. Pair Extraordinaire!   (3:17)
11. My Well-Tempered Broadwood   (4:19)
12. 'O Love As Long As You Can!'   (5:23)
13. The Known Great Composer   (4:25)
14. The JOH. SEB. Bach Limericks   (2:14)
15. Ludwig van Beethoven   (4:13)
16. A Natural Virtuoso!   (5:24)

Duration 71:26

All poems have been written and performed by Michael Bobb

Music by: Mozart, Schubert, Ponchielli, Saint-Saëns, Beethoven,
Traditional/Michael Bobb, Chopin, Debussy, Liszt, J. S. Bach

All rights reserved
© Michael Bobb   Produced AD 2020
www.michaelbobb.com

Audiobook on YouTube

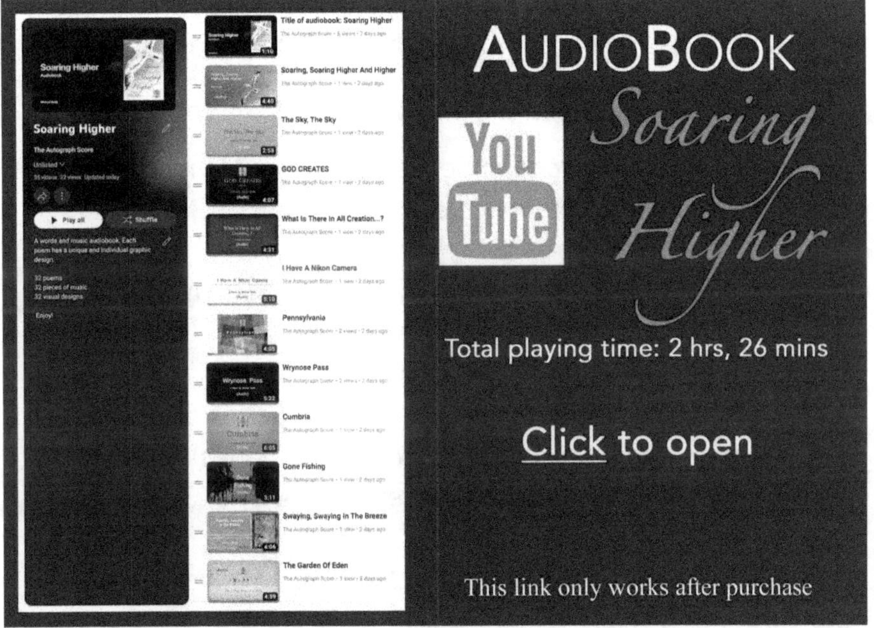

Available from

The Autograph Score

www.theautographscore.co.uk

Music in audiobook

1. Soaring, Soaring Higher And Higher *(Edvard Grieg – Morning Mood from Peer Gynt Suite No. 1)*

2. The Sky, The Sky *(Johann Sebastian Bach – Menuett In G from the Anna Magdalena Notenbüchlein)*

3. GOD CREATES *(George Frideric Handel – Suite No. 4 in D Minor, HWV 437, Sarabande)*

4. What Is There In All Creation…? *(Johann Sebastian Bach – Prelude 1 from The Forty-Eight Preludes and Fugues) (Charles Gounod – Ave Maria based on the first Prelude by J. S. Bach)*

5. I Have A Nikon Camera *(Johann Sebastian Bach – Bourrée from Violin Partita No. 1)*

6. Pennsylvania *(Antonin Dvorák – Themes from The New World Symphony)*

7. Wrynose Pass *(Ludwig van Beethoven – Sonata Quasi Una Fantasia, Op. 27, No. 2, "Moonlight")*

8. Cumbria *(Sir Peter Maxwell Davies – Farewell To Stromness)*

9. Gone Fishing *(Franz Schubert – The Trout)*

10. Swaying, Swaying In The Breeze *(Ludwig van Beethoven – Sonate Pathétique, Op. 13, Adagio Cantabile)*

11. The Garden Of Eden *(Ronald Binge – Elizabethan Serenade)*

12. This Is The Month – Eastertide *(George Frideric Handel – I Know That My Redeemer Liveth from Messiah)*

13. My Peace *(Erik Satie – Gymnopédie No. 1)*

14. The Ultimate Renewed Environment *(Ludwig van Beethoven – Andante Con Moto from Fifth Symphony)*

15. A Natural Virtuoso! *(Johann Sebastian Bach – Toccata from Toccata And Fugue in D Minor, BWV 565)*

16. The Known Great Composer *(Johann Sebastian Bach – Cello Suite III, Bourrée)*

17. The JOH. SEB. Bach Limericks *(Johann Sebastian Bach – Fugue from Toccata And Fuque in D Minor, BWV 565)*

18. Ludwig van Beethoven *(Ludwig van Beethoven – Ode To Joy from Symphony No. 9)*

19. "O Love As Long As You Can!" *(Franz Liszt – "O Lieb So Lang Du Lieben Kannst")*

20. My Well-Tempered Broadwood *(Ludwig van Beethoven – Sonata Op. 28, Scherzo, "Pastorale")*

21. Avril's New Car *(Wolfgang Amadeus Mozart – Rondo from Sonata in C, K545)*

22. Mr Spock And The Lost Left Sock *(Camille Saint-Saëns – The Elephant from The Carnival Of The Animals)*

23. Billy-Nilly *(Franz Schubert – Trio from Scherzo No. 2)*

24. High Street! (Outside In, Inside Out) *(Amilcare Ponchielli – Dance Of The Hours from La Gioconda)*

25. Saffron And Wine Lamb *(Ludwig van Beethoven – Minuet in G)*

26. Dear Maiden, Fair Maiden *(Traditional/Michael Bobb – Scarborough Fair)*

27. Pair Extraordinaire! *(Claude Debussy – La Fille Aux Cheveux De Lin from Préludes Book 1)*

28. Where Would The Summer Be…? *(Frédéric Chopin – Berceuse, Op. 57)*

29. The Greeting Kiss *(Traditional – Greensleeves)*

30. The Parting Kiss *(Johann Pachelbel – Canon in D)*

31. Summer Rain *(Frédéric Chopin – Prelude In D Flat, Op. 28, No. 15, "Raindrop")*

32. Images: Pictures In My Mind *(Modest Mussorgskij – Promenade from Bilder Einer Ausstellung)*

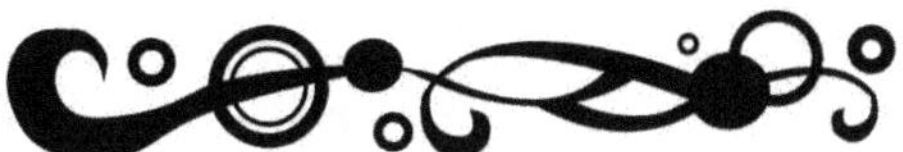